The New Guitar

Written by
Rob Waring and **Maurice Jamall**

Before You Read

to break
(broken)

floor

to clean
something

glue

to drop
something

guitar

to fix
something

keyboard

to jump

money

band

rock star

drums

table

dirty

In the story

Ray

Eric

Mr. Walker

"They are really good," thinks Ray.
He is watching his friends play in their band.
They are playing music at Eric's house.
Eric plays the guitar. Kenji plays the drums, and Yoon-Hee plays the keyboard.
Ray thinks, "I want to play, too, but I don't have a guitar."

Today it is Ray's birthday. He wants a guitar.
He wants to play the guitar in Eric's band.
He is with his father. His father is looking for a guitar
for Ray's birthday.
They go to the music store. Ray's friend Eric comes, too.
He knows about guitars.

Ray says to his father, "Dad, please buy me this guitar. It's really good!"

Ray's father asks Eric about the guitar.

"Eric, I don't know about guitars. Is this a good guitar, Eric?" he asks.

Eric tells Ray's father about the guitar. "No, it's not a good guitar."

Ray says, "But I want it, Dad. It's great!"

"No, don't buy it, Ray. It's no good," says Eric.

Ray's father says, "Ray, I'm sorry, but I'm not buying it for you."

Ray says, "But . . . Dad. Please!"

"I'm sorry, no," he says. Ray's father buys him a book about guitars.

"Thanks, Dad," Ray says. But he is not happy. He really wants the guitar.

Ray thinks, "I can buy it with *my* money!"

The next day, Ray gets his money from his room.
He goes to the music store. He gives the guitar to the man.
"Can I have this guitar, please?" he says.
Ray buys the guitar. He has no money now, but he is very happy.
He does not tell his mother and father.

Ray goes to Eric's house.
"Eric, look!" says Ray. "I have the guitar now. Do you like it?"
He shows the guitar to Eric.
Eric does not like Ray's guitar. "This isn't a good guitar, Ray,"
says Eric. Ray is not happy, but he wants to play in the band.
Eric looks at Ray. Then he smiles. "Come on, Ray, let's make
some music."

Ray is very happy. Now he can play in the band.
Ray plays the guitar with the band. He is not good, but he likes playing the guitar.
He wants to be a good guitarist.
"This is really great," he thinks. "I love my new guitar!"
The music is not good, but everybody is having a good time.

Ray wants to be a rock star. He likes the band, Dark Sun.
Eric, Kenji, Yoon-Hee, and Ray play many songs.
Ray loves playing his new guitar with the band.
He is not good at playing the guitar, but he is having a
good time. He thinks he is in the band, Dark Sun.

Ray gets very excited. He jumps with his guitar.
But he drops it, and his guitar breaks.
"Oh, no! My guitar! It's broken!" Ray says.
Everybody looks at his guitar. He cannot play music now.
Ray thinks, "What do I do now?"

Ray goes home with his guitar. He wants to fix it. He wants to play it again. He gets some things to fix the guitar. He puts them on the table.

He thinks, "I don't want Mom and Dad to see the broken guitar."

Ray wants to fix the guitar, but he is not very good at fixing things.
"How do I fix it?" he thinks. He looks at his guitar book.
Ray tries to fix the guitar, but he cannot.
"Oh no!" he thinks.

The cat jumps on the table. Some glue goes on the table. "Oh no!" says Ray. The cat walks in the glue. Now glue is everywhere, too.

Ray tries to stop the cat, but he drops the guitar again. It breaks again.

"My guitar!" he says. He is very angry with the cat.

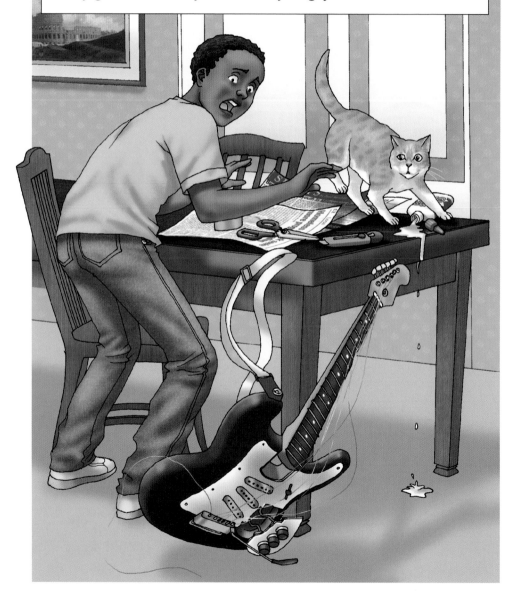

The cat jumps down and walks on the floor. Now the floor is dirty, too.

"Oh, no! The floor!" says Ray.

Ray tries to clean the table. But the table is very dirty.

He tries to clean the floor. But he is not good at cleaning.

Ray's mother and father come home.
"Ray! What's this on the table?" asks his mother.
"And what's this on the floor?"
"What's this guitar doing here?" asks his father.
Ray looks at them and says nothing. He is in trouble now.